WITHDRAWN

TREES AND SHRUBS
For Small Gardens

Today is the age of the small garden. This book has been specially written for those gardeners wishing to make the best possible use of the limited space they have available, with the minimum amount of time to expend on it. Full cultural details are given together with complete lists of suitable shrubs and trees.

TREES AND SHRUBS
FOR SMALL GARDENS

By

A. G. PUTTOCK

MAGNA PRINT BOOKS
LITTON . YORKSHIRE

LARGE TYPE EDITION

635.97
P993t

First Published in large print 1975
by
Magna Print Books
Litton, Skipton, Yorkshire
by arrangement with
W. & G. Foyle Limited
London

© Large Print Edition 1975
Magna Print Books

ISBN 0 86009 034 5

Contents

Foreword

1 The Approach 9

2 The Soil and its Preparation 15

3 Planting 23

4 Propagation 30

5 Spring Flowering Species 43

6 Early Summer Species 61

7 Late Summer Species 81

8 Autumn and Winter Species 96

9 Hedges 101

10 Climbers and Wall Shrubs 109

11 Landscaping 113

CHAPTER I

The Approach

THE BEAUTIES of flowering shrubs and trees have been enjoyed in our gardens for just about four hundred years. It is probable that Lavender and Laburnum, which came from the European Mediterranean, were amongst the first to be imported. These were followed by a number of the more popular subjects such as Jasmine, Almond, Apricot and Nectarine.

Early in 1600 a number of plants were introduced from returning voyages of discovery. These included the Judas Tree, Lilac, Mock Orange and Laurustinus.

Importations continued at regular intervals but there is little record of actual dates until the early eighteenth century when we received the first Magnolias, the first Ceanothus and the Mountain Laurel. The remainder of the century brought a comparatively large number of other new species, including the Camellia, Tree Paeony,

Yulan, Japonica, Aucuba, Fuchsia and others.

The nineteenth century brought further species including Wisteria, Kerria Japonica, Rhododendron, Snowberry, Flowering Currant, Garrya, Cotoneaster and very many others.

It was not really until 1860 onwards that the true potentialities of flowering shrubs were fully realised. At one time they were restricted entirely to large gardens, partly through the dictates of expense and partly owing to the fact that the cottage garden was necessarily devoted almost entirely to the production of food.

Now, however, the large-scale garden, requiring a large staff of gardeners for its upkeep, has very nearly disappeared. Conversely the number of gardens and gardeners has very greatly increased; but it is noticeable that the gardeners are now amateur and not professional. Whether one's garden is small or spacious it has become vitally necessary to economise in labour and for this reason alone the trend has been towards flowering trees and shrubs instead of the more usual formal or informal bedding schemes with flowers.

Shrubs and trees are both woody perennial plants, each with a life span of from several to many years. A shrub is a plant with woody stems branching freely and abundantly from or near the base. A tree is a woody plant with a single main stem or trunk rising from the ground, bearing lateral branches.

Flowering trees and shrubs present a galaxy that is both varied and replete with interest. They number among them evergreen and deciduous species, tall, medium and dwarf varieties, upright, spreading and weeping forms. In addition to the varied nature of the general picture they present, they have the outstanding characteristic offered by no other garden plants, which I touched on above; once established, they require little labour for their maintenance. They do, however, require for their correct and efficient employment, a basic knowledge of their character, size and requirements. It is for this reason and with the object of helping the many small gardeners, to whom labour saving may well be a vital problem, that this book has been compiled.

Since shrubs and trees nowadays form such an important feature in the modern garden — and are likely to increase even further in popularity — it is essential that one should be fully conversant with their merits and disadvantages from the start. This will help considerably in the selection of the right subject for the right place. They are the dominant plants in a garden and for this reason must be considered individually and not as a mass as one considers the plants of, say, a herbaceous border or rock garden. On the other hand it is equally essential to consider the mass in the form of the finished picture, so that one can group the various species correctly in association one with another. In this way their individual characteristics will stand out to the best advantage whatever the season.

One must remember that the full beauty of the flowering shrub and tree will not be apparent for five or even ten years after planting and allowance must be made for this fact. Furthermore, the flowers, however beautiful, do not provide the sole merit of these plants. However, it is a fact that one of the chief criticisms that has been levelled against shrubs and trees is their dull aspect when not in flower. This is quite untrue and consequently it is advisable to consider the question of foliage as being equally as important as the actual flowers, or very nearly so.

There is another feature which will add to the aesthetic beauty of a shrub or tree and this is its shape. The question of successful planting to provide a beautiful landscape, however small, is a secret which must also be mastered.

In the small shrub garden, symmetry of effect deserves little commendation. Nothing can be quite so dull as a border planted to slope from a straight line at the back, to a similar but less elevated line at the front. Thus it is necessary to consider initially how far diversity of contour is desirable and to select one's subjects with this end in view, using taller-growing varieties either as a background for contrasting species, as a means to hide some architectural hideosity in sight of one's house and/or garden or to provide partial shade for those species which do not require full sunlight. This will be discussed in more detail in Chapter 11; at this stage it is enough to realise that these points must be considered.

Finally, one must not forget the question of the climate. Many of our most delightful flowering shrubs and trees were originally imported from rather more generous conditions than our own. Even so, the majority of them, and certainly those I recommend in these pages, are basically looked upon as hardy. It is only fair to say, however, that some species which will flourish in Devon and Cornwall will not survive in the colder Northern counties of Britain. Others will be intolerant of winds — in particular those sometimes found near our coastline. Frost pockets too must be avoided, as the conditions sometime prevailing in habitual frost pockets will seal the doom of many of our hardiest plants. In the same way, the Western counties are wetter and warmer than the Eastern counties and allowance must be made for this fact. The nearness of a garden to a city, town or industrial area will also greatly affect the quality of our trees and shrubs. Industrial smog will reduce the quality and amount of sunshine they receive and will also cause filth to be deposited on both flowers and foliage. Such conditions will deny us the use of many of the finer species in the town garden.

CHAPTER II

The Soil and its Preparation

WHEN classifying soils with any degree of detail one uses such divisions as sandy, clay, silt, chalk, loam, marl, and even 'building site' soil; it is as well for the reader to have a passing glimpse of what is meant by each.

A sandy soil is one in which the soil particles include as much as 70% of sand. These can be identified by picking up a handful of moist soil and rubbing it between thumb and forefinger. It will feel gritty.

A clay soil is one in which 30% or over, by weight, of its particles are clay. These are particles of less than .002 mms. in diameter. A clay soil can be identified by its generally wet and 'heavy' appearance. It will frequently be yellow in colour and a handful will feel sticky.

A silt soil is one that is made up of the finer sand particles, together with a proportion of clay. To handle it will feel of a silky texture.

A chalky soil is one which generally lies on top of chalk or limestone, though this is not essential. It can frequently be identified by the predominance of small white, chalky particles in the soil.

A loam is a mixture of clay, sand or silt and fully decayed organic matter, known as humas. Loams vary and may be described as clay loam, sandy loam, light loam, heavy loam etc. In some parts of the country, 'loam' is the name given to the top few inches of soil remaining after a covering of turf has been removed.

A marl is the name given to a chalky loam.

A 'building site' soil may consist of anything. It is what is left behind after the builders have finished. The subsoil excavated from the foundations will generally have been spread around on top of the original top-soil. It may contain brick-bats, scrap-iron, mortar particles and many other ingredients. Invariably it will be completely infertile as it is.

Having filed the details of the various soils in the depths of our mind we can now divide them for purposes of growing trees and shrubs into two main headings, acid and alkaline.

The acid content of the soil is measured by a special scale known as the pH scale. This scale is based on the Hydrogen Ion Concentration (HIC) per unit volume. The pH of pure water, (H,OH) which on dissociation provides an equal number of both Hydrogen and Hydroxyl Ions (OH) and therefore neutral is 7.07 (The content of Hydroxyl Ions is ignored). Thus neutral pH is taken at the round figure of seven. By adding acid to pure water one increases the acidity or HIC but, owing to the method of calculation, it lowers the pH value. Conversely, by adding a substance dissociating to yield OH one lowers the HIC and raises the pH. The pH scale thus extends upwards and downwards from the neutral figure of seven. A pH more than seven denotes alkalinity. It is an interesting fact in passing that many of the beautiful colours in plants, both of flowers and foliage, are due to substances which indicate a change in HIC.

The majority of soils over the greater part of the British Isles are acid soils with a pH value of between 5.5 and 6.5. This is indeed fortunate because the majority of our plants require slightly acid conditions.

One must not confuse an acid soil with a sour soil. The latter arises where the soil is so tightly packed or waterlogged that the soil atmosphere is driven out. The soil life, composed of teeming organisms essential to fertility, cannot therefore exist.

The acidity and alkalinity of any soil can be varied in proportion to the pH value. Thus at pH 6 the alkalinity is ten times greater than at pH 5 and at pH 7 it is 100 times greater. It follows therefore that the higher the pH the more acid reacting material has to be used to neutralise alkalinity. In practice it is only an economic proposition to make an alkaline soil more acid when the pH is not more than seven, and when the soil is sufficiently light to react to moderate doses of acid reacting materials.

The following materials may be used to induce acidity: peat, oak-leaf-mould, composted pine needles, sulphur and aluminium sulphate.

Where it is desired to change an acid soil to alkaline, the addition of calcium in some form and in quantities according to the requirement will do all that is necessary.

From time to time the pH of a soil that has been altered in character should be checked over as the tendency will always be to return to its normal, original composition.

It is a strange fact that the ideal soil for shrubs

and trees is generally that which is present in one's neighbours garden and seldom that to be found on one's own piece of land. It is a good light loam, free of lime and well drained. This ideal will seldom be found as such and we must therefore consider how it can be secured.

In its natural state soil contains:

Mineral Matter
Organic Matter
Water
Gases
Bacteria

The mineral matter is derived from rocks and forms by far the largest constituent in ordinary soils. The organic matter represents the remains chiefly of decaying vegetable and animal matter and is referred to as humus. The water is received from the clouds as rain or by drainage from higher land or by irrigation. The gases enter by diffusion from the air above or are manufactured within the soil. All healthy soils contain bacteria which play an extremely important part in the production of nitrates which the plant can absorb readily.

Returning once more to the method of producing the most suitable soil for growing trees and shrubs. Clay soils and clay loams can be improved by liming, which causes the soil to flocculate or gather together in larger particles with the consequent improvement in drainage. Alternatively, if one does not wish to alter the pH — as one will be adding lime — one can add any coarse organic or inorganic material such as coarse sand, boiler-ash, leaf mould or peat.

Sandy soils and sandy loams will be characterised by their inability to hold water. These can be improved by the addition of peat, leaf mould, farmyard manure, compost or, in fact, any forms of humus.

In the case of chalky soils the answer is largely the same. The incorporation of humus in order to increase the surface tillage will generally achieve the desired result.

Many of the poorer soils will require a dressing of manure or fertiliser. This must be provided in order to supply the growing plant with the requisite food. This again must be supplied in a balanced form and will consist of proportionate amounts of Nitrogen, Phosphorus, Potash and Calcium and the part played by these constituents must be clearly understood.

Nitrogen plays an important part in the build-up

of the plant and is responsible for shoot and leaf growth. In adequate supply it ensures healthy, rich-coloured foliage and strong shoot growth, though an excess of it may produce over-luxuriant, soft growth.

Phosphorus provides the energy and fruitfulness of the plant. Root development is dependent on it from seedling to the mature state.

Potash is the growth balancer. It is equivalent to the salt which savours the food of humans. It encourages firm growth, thus counter-balancing the tendency of nitrogen to produce softness and luxuriance. Potash also gives brilliance to flower colours which may otherwise be lacking.

Calcium in addition to its properties as an ant-acid, is an essential plant food and it plays its part in the formation of cell tissues.

When a soil is prepared for planting flowering trees and shrubs it will generally have a proportion of these four elements added in the form of an organic manure, such as farmyard manure, or organic fertiliser such as fish manure, National Growmore or one of the other proprietary products. Subsequent dressings will be provided in the form of a mulch.

The mulch has been used in British gardens

for a very great number of years but only in a small way. Recently however the practice of mulching the whole garden is spreading from the United States of America.

The advantage of a mulch of this sort is that it provides a dressing for the soil, it reduces the growth of weeds and the consequent necessity for cultivation — thus saving labour and reducing the chance of damaging shallow rooted plants — and it keeps the roots cool and moist.

Materials which can be used for mulching purposes include sawdust, lawn mowings, well rotted manure, home made compost, peat, wood wool and straw, though some of these materials are obviously preferable to others, dependent on their usefulness and relative unsightliness.

Mulches are spread round the plants or over the whole bed in autumn and/or spring.

CHAPTER III

Planting

IT IS perhaps rather putting the cart before the horse to discuss planting — or more correctly, *trans*planting — before the propagation of trees and shrubs, but, as most amateur gardeners purchase their plants, initially at any rate, from a nursery it is, I think, better to adopt this order.

Transplanting is an ordeal for any shrub or tree and for this reason they should be moved as little as possible. The symptoms displayed by any shrubs which have been moved frequently are somewhat stunted growth and short joints, and if a preference can be made it will be this type of plant which the knowledgeable gardener selects as being likely to move well.

It is a far more hazardous operation to transplant evergreens and conifers than the deciduous type of plants, and for this reason they are taken with as large a ball of soil as possible so as to occasion the minimum root disturbance as possible. Where this is not possible it is essential to choose the correct time of year for the move. With the evergreen there is no period of leaf-fall to compensate for the ruthless curtailment of the root system and the fall in supply of moisture from the roots is felt more considerably than in the case of deciduous shrubs. It is therefore essential that the root system should not be disturbed when it is at its slowest period of development, but only when it is most likely to make immediate growth. For this reason, it is generally preferable to move evergreens and conifers during the warm, showery weather generally experienced in April and May. This must be followed by the precautions necessary to ensure that sufficient water is given during the following summer to avoid allowing any part of the root system to dry out.

An alternative season for moving this type of shrub or tree is the months of September or October, once again, providing that the weather is warm and showery. The actual times will vary slightly between the North and South of the country as it does for cultural operations for any horticultural subject.

Where it is desired to move a larger and more

fully established tree or shrub there must be a period of preparation of at least one and perhaps two years beforehand. The root system will be much larger in this case and it is obvious that if all the roots were severed and the shrub moved to a new home there would be little, if any, chance of survival. In this case the size of the ball is marked out, and a trench is dug just inside the measured space, to such a depth that all the roots are severed, for a distance of half way round the shrub. The ball is then undermined to cut any tap roots, the soil replaced, the trench filled in and plenty of water given. In some cases the other half of the ball may then be similarly treated, but in the case of the larger and more valuable shrubs this should be done during the following season.

When purchasing trees and shrubs from a reputable nurseryman these will always be supplied at the correct season of the year. They will have been lifted correctly, packed carefully and sent by the most expeditious means. On arrival arrangements must be made to carry out the planting operation as soon as possible, though a delay of a day or so will not cause any damage. If, for any reason, it is necessary to delay for more than a couple of days the sacking or straw surrounding the roots of the newly arrived shrubs and trees should be well watered and this will protect them from drying out.

It is always advantageous to purchase shrubs and trees when they are as small as possible, and exercise a degree of patience with regard to their growth; there are, however, certain species, including particularly the Rhododendrons, which will move very well even when larger and older.

It is assumed that the bed in which the shrubs are to be planted will have been prepared some time before their arrival. The next step therefore is to prepare each individual site. In this operation one must dig the correct holes, and they must be deep enough and wide enough to take the root systems comfortably. The subsoil must be well forked over and have a proportion of fertiliser incorporated in with it.

Where it is proposed to plant an acid loving plant in an alkaline soil and *vice versa*, the holes must be treated either with aluminium sulphate or lime. The top soil to be used to refill each hole must be carefully prepared, incorporating any further supplies of peat, compost, leaf-mould, etc. that is needed and once again this will have to be prepared according to the acid or alkaline requirements of the plants.

The exact positioning of the plant in the soil as regards depth and most favourable aspect insofar as the branches are concerned is of paramount importance. If too deep the surface roots cannot get the air they need to function properly and basal buds may not be able to burst into new shoots; if too shallow there will be a very real danger of frost. As regards the aspect, it is obviously preferable to position a shrub or tree to provide most of its beauty for its owners, rather than for their neighbours.

The roots must then be carefully laid out in their natural positions, radiating outwards and downwards from the base of the stem or trunk. Friable soil is firmed about them and gradually the planting process proceeds. The whole operation must be conducted with gentleness and never should such a tool as a rammer be used. Finally a protective mulch must be placed round the base of the stem or trunk.

It is very often necessary to provide a stake for a newly planted tree or shrub, particularly in a site that is exposed to the wind. A strong stake of suitable size is given a sharp tapered point; this is then tapped into place with the tree or shrub standing in the hole but before the top soil is replaced. In this way the stake can be positioned without causing damage to the root system. As soon as the planting operation is completed, a piece of doubled sacking is wrapped round the tree at a level some six inches below the top of the stake. An adequate length of galvanised wire is then placed round the tree (over the sacking) and round the stake in a figure-of-eight and firmly secured. Such a tie will hold the tree firmly in place for so long as it is required or so long as the stake lasts. It should be inspected each year and loosened slightly as the stem or trunk thickens with age. It is possible to obtain plastic ties for use instead of wire though these are more expensive and no more satisfactory.

As each shrub or tree is planted it is a wise plan to affix a special plant label to each giving full particulars of genus, species and variety and the date of planting. It may also be advantageous, if plants have been obtained from a number of different nurseries to add the origin of each in addition to the more usual information.

It is often after planting has been carried out that the plant is subjected to the greatest dangers by way of cold winds, drying soil, etc., and it is at this stage that plants have the least amount of resistance to such conditions. In event of there being a spell of cold winds it is advisable to erect a temporary screen of hurdles, hessian, etc., as a wind break. Dry soils can only be countered by means of a regular watering curriculum and it is often helpful to incorporate a proportion of liquid manure with this, thus providing a very weak feed at the same time.

The problems arising from the spacing of plants is dealt with in Chapter XI, under the heading of 'Landscaping'.

CHAPTER IV

Propagation

THERE will almost certainly come a time when all amateur gardeners will want to try their hand at propagation. Eventually this urge may well spread to flowering trees and shrubs. These may be reproduced in the following way:

(a) by seeds
(b) by division
(c) by layering
(d) by cuttings, stem, root or leaf
(e) by budding or grafting.

Some species do not reproduce themselves accurately from seeds and must be propagated by one of the vegetative means. This applies particularly to 'Sports' and those of contorted, fastigiate or weeping habits. These types are seldom found in nature and rely on the human element for their continued existence. There are also a number of species which will not even produce fertile seeds in their own native lands. These too must be reproduced vegetatively.

Species which can be relied upon to produce fertile seeds are best reproduced in this way as they will provide clean, healthy stock.

Seed Sowing

It must be understood from the start that there are so many different types of seed from the different species of trees and shrubs that it is impossible to standardise a single method for sowing seeds, owing to the wide difference in size, shape and texture. Take for example the difference between the 'conker' of a Horse Chestnut and the minute seeds of a Fuchsia.

Let us consider first of all the small seeds. The receptacles to be used may be either seed boxes or pots, and the choice really revolves round the number of seeds to be sown. The boxes or pots must be washed and disinfected, a solution of Permanganate of Potash probably being the best general disinfectant for the purpose.

The soil in which the seeds are to be sown must be made up of sterilised soil, and the standard John Innes Seed Compost will be the most useful. This is made up of: 2 parts sterilised loam, 1 part granulated peat, 1 part sand, all mixed by bulk.

Then to each bushel of the compost is added ¾ oz. ground chalk or lime-stone and 1½ oz. superphosphate. (The ground chalk should be omitted in the case of seeds of plants which require an acid soil.)

The seed receptacles should be crocked and filled up with soil in the normal manner prescribed for any other seeds.

The larger seeds are sprinkled finely or separately positioned over the surface of the soil and a sprinkling of fine soil, about one-sixteenth of an inch in depth, should be provided as a covering. In the case of small seeds the process is similar but a covering of fine moss is preferable to soil.

The receptacles are then placed in an open frame or in a sheltered part of the garden in partial shade. Watering should be carried out by the process of partial immersion. A pinch of permanganate of potash may be added to the water to help guard against damping off.

The seeds of shrubs and trees should be sown as soon as they are ripe. Some of the tougher types of seeds may be soaked for twenty-four hours before sowing with advantage.

Once germination has taken place and the

little plants are large enough to handle, the seedlings should be pricked out. This should be in the early spring. Progress will very soon be observed if the seedlings are going ahead. If no progress is observed a further batch may be pricked out. For this reason it is advisable not to disturb the seed boxes more than necessary when pricking out the first batch.

Seedlings may be pricked out into pots filled with John Innes Potting Compost No. 1, or into a nursery bed and given the temporary protection of a cold-frame, or of a few cloches. The John Innes No. 1 Compost is made up of: 7 parts sterilised loam, 3 parts granulated peat, 2 parts sand, all mixed by bulk. To each bushel of the mixture add ¾ oz. ground chalk or lime stone and 4 oz. John Innes Base.* (The ground chalk should be omitted in the case of subjects requiring an acid soil.)

Seedlings planted into a nursery bed should be provided with a removable, slatted cover so that they can be partially shaded when necessary, and plenty of moisture should be provided at all times without waterlogging the soil.

* Note. John Innes Base is made up of 2 parts Hoof and Horn (1/8 grist) 2 parts superphosphate and 1 part Sulphate of Potash — all by weight.

Root Division

This is by far the simplest method of reproduction and it merely consists of pulling suitable plants apart into separate pieces or stems, each with roots attached, and replanting them. If the roots of one or more sections are not very well developed on division they should be replanted into a sandy compost to encourage further root growth before there is much advance in top growth. This method can be practised with those shrubs of a tufted habit, producing sucker growths or shoots from below the surface of the soil and include *Berberis darwinii*, Kerria, Deutzia, Diervilla, Symphoricarpos and Spiraea. Division should be carried out in the early spring.

Layering

There are now two methods of layering — the old-fashioned method of ground layering and the more modern method of air layering.

A layer is a shoot or branch of a plant which is induced to root before being cut off. It is a method which can be adopted for practically all species of trees and shrubs but in practice it is generally restricted to shrubs having supple branches near the ground which can be pegged to the soil, or to shrubs which are difficult to increase by any other means.

The usual method of ground layering consists of bending a suitable branch and then notching or slitting the stem or removing a narrow strip of bark round the circumference of the stem at the lowest point of the bend in order to interrupt the flow of sap. The next step is to peg down the piece of stem so treated and cover it with a mound of good loam. The terminal end must be turned more or less upright and secured to a stake. This will eventually form the basis of the new plant.

Layering of this sort is best carried out in April or May before the new growth begins. The shoot should then stand for twelve months before being severed; it is then lifted with roots and soil intact and planted on its own.

Air layering is a method of propagation which has been practised for many years but the old method was so cumbersome that it was not often employed. The modern method is vastly more simple, and air layering is now looked upon as being comparatively easy. A suitable shoot with healthy firm wood is chosen and a ring of bark approximately one inch wide removed. The point of the ring is at once enclosed in a ball of thoroughly damp sphagnum moss and then covered round with a specially treated sheet of polythene. This can be purchased already impregnated with the necessary plant foods and root inducing hormones. This is tied in place at each end and in a few weeks roots will be sufficiently developed to allow the detachment of the layer for potting into a good rooting compost for growing on as a separate plant.

Cuttings

Cuttings provide the most important method of propagation in the case of shrubs but, though the method may be used with some success in the case of many species of tree, it cannot be claimed to do so with certainty.

The difference between a cutting and a layer is the fact that a cutting is completely detached from the parent plant whereas, as has been seen above, a layer is not so detached until rooting has taken place. For this reason the propagator must be capable of keeping the cutting alive until such time as the plant is in a position to look after itself. Thus dormant or hard-wood cuttings which have no leaves with which to transpire can be kept alive for a very long time; for this reason they will generally root perfectly easily in the open, though the process will take longer than with green cuttings. Green or soft-wood cuttings, which are generally taken during the summer months, are usually generously provided with leaves with which to transpire and they must be provided with a moist atmosphere and sufficient encouragement by way of temperature to promote a rapid process of rooting. For this reason green cuttings are best provided with a close, moist atmosphere and partial shade so that transpiration is not too rapid. In this way flagging, which is so detrimental to a cutting, can be avoided.

The question of taking cuttings is one that can only be mastered with experience. The expert knows exactly which are the best shoots to take. Generally speaking one avoids the leading shoot and selects a side branch which is not too leafy and which may be anything from three to five inches in length. The ripeness of the wood is important when hard-wood cuttings are concerned and will naturally vary according to the seasonal climatic conditions. Cuttings should be taken as soon as the wood is ripe.

Very frequently, cuttings will be more satisfactory if taken with a heel of the old wood. In other words, the new season's growth is taken at a point where it joins the old growth, by means of a sharp downward tug; this will allow a heel of the old wood to come away too. If the heel is ragged it should be trimmed smooth with a sharp knife or razor blade.

Unless taken with a heel of old wood, cuttings should be severed with a sharp, clean, straight cut through the shoot, just below a node or leaf joint.

They should then be inserted into a good cuttings compost made up of: 1 part sterilised loam, 2 parts peat, 1 part sand, all mixed by bulk, except those destined for the cold frame or the open ground when a normal soil is used with the addition of some silver sand.

Root formation can be expedited by the use of one of the synthetic growth-promoting substances or hormones. It must however be clearly under-stood that hormones will not produce roots on a cutting that is incorrectly taken.

Transpiration can be checked by spraying cuttings with the new plastic spray material S600 and this will allow many soft-wood cuttings to be propagated in the open.

Certain shrubs can be propagated from root cuttings, consisting of three inch lengths of root, about a quarter of an inch thick, placed upright in a cuttings compost or sandy soil, with the part of the root nearest the stem at soil level. These are taken in March or April and it is simpler to use a propagating frame for the purpose.

Leaf cuttings are not normally used for propagating trees and shrubs except in the case of Camellias. Here a cutting consists of a leaf, its bud and a small piece of stem. It is taken in March and inserted in a sandy compost in a propagating frame with slight bottom heat.

Budding

This is a form of grafting in which a bud of the selected plant is used as the scion, or the top growth. The operation is carried out in July or August and is used principally in the reproduction of Roses, Flowering Cherries and some of the better types of Rhododendron, Magnolia and Viburnum. The stock, or root part of the plant, will naturally depend on the genus. In the case of Lilac the common *Syringa vulgaris* is used, for Cherry the wild native Gean (*Prunus avium*) is very satisfactory, etc.

The correct method of budding is to choose wood buds from firm, well-ripened shoots of the current year's growth. These are detached by means of a sharp knife on the long, thin shield of bark and wood, commencing the cut half an inch above the bud and ending the same distance below. The woody part on the reverse side is then carefully removed, without damaging or removing the inside of the bud, and leaving a greenish-white slippery surface exposed.

The stock is made ready to receive the bud by making a T-shaped cut about one and a half inches in length and half an inch across the top, on a clean, smooth part of the bark, so that the bark can be lifted sufficiently to allow the pre-pared bud to be slipped inside. The bark is pressed back and the bud is securely tied in place with raffia, leaving the actual eye of the bud exposed. As an additional precaution grafting wax may be placed over the wound, once again ensuring that the eye is left clear. When the bud begins to swell the fastening material must be loosened and the top of the stock, above the bud, removed.

Budding should be done in dull weather or in the early morning. If carried out late in the season the bud may remain dormant until the following spring.

Grafting

This is an unwieldy method of reproduction which was vastly more favoured by our parents and grandparents than by ourselves, though it is still essential in the case of some species.

Sometimes it is possible to grow a more robust plant by grafting but generally speaking they are seldom superior to those grown on their own roots.

The key to successful grafting lies in placing the cambium layers of both stock and scion in intimate contact with each other, and with the exclusion of air.

The stocks to be used for grafting are generally grown from seed or by means of cuttings until the stems are about half an inch in diameter. Grafting is carried out in April or May. The simplest method is to cut both stock and scion with a slanting cut so that they can be fitted together, fasten them with raffia and smear the joint with grafting wax to exclude air. With the cambium layers in close contact, the stock and scion unite and when the scion is seen to be making new growth the raffia is cut to allow the stem to expand.

Other types of graft include the 'Whip and Tongue' graft, the 'saddle' graft, or the 'rind' graft which is only used when the size of the stock greatly exceeds that of the scion.

* Note. John Innes Base is made up of 2 parts Hoof and Horn (1/8 grist) 2 parts super-phosphate and 1 part Sulphate of Potash — all by weight.

CHAPTER V

Spring Flowering Species

February to April

AFTER the rigours of winter no one can fail to be moved by the glories of the spring flowering shrubs and trees. They come at a time when there is little else in the garden and even the early daffodils have little more than begun to push up their buds.

The choice includes some of the most valuable species, such as Magnolia, Camellia and the Tree Paeony, and also some of the commonest and least expensive.

The difficulty, when making a shrub garden, is to choose enough of these spring beauties without overcrowding the garden and thus having little or nothing to follow for the rest of the year.

Let us now select a number of the most delightful species and give a little information about each one. *Amelanchier canadensis* is a lovely little tree growing to some 20 ft. in height. During April it is virtually covered with white blossom as a result of which it is sometimes known as the 'Snowy Mespilus'. In autumn the foliage turns to a rich red or yellow and thus provides a double issue of colour which is particularly acceptable in the small garden. It is not particular as to soil but prefers slight acidity. Reproduction is carried out by means of seeds sown in February or cuttings in July. It will require some 15 ft. in diameter in which to spread when fully grown.

Azalea mollis should correctly be called *Rhododendron × molle* but because the family is generally known as Azalea I am classifying it under that name. It is a hybrid offspring from *Rhododendron japonicum* and the genuine *R. molle*. It is one of the most beautiful of all garden shrubs and possesses a wide range of colours. It is certainly very suitable for the small garden. It needs a lime-free, open soil, in a sheltered, partially shaded part of the garden. Some plants are grafted, but generally speaking they are best when grown on their own roots. They should be planted ten feet apart. No pruning is necessary, but well shaped plants growing on their own roots will send up shoots from the base. These may be arched over and pegged down and flower buds will form all along the shoots. Seed pods must also be removed. Some of the best varieties include Adrian Koster (deep yellow), Floradora (orange), Clara Butt (deep pink), Mrs. Oliver Slocock (orange-yellow), J. C. Van Thol (red), Marmion (pale yellow, deeper flare), Mrs. G. A. van Moordt (salmon).

Berberis. There are so many species of this genus which are ideally suited to the small garden that it is difficult to select a few of the best. More species will be discussed later under the heading of Mahonia. All prefer an alkaline soil.

B. buxifolia is a Chilean species, with box-like leaves, which is sometimes known as *B. dulcis.* Flowering in April, it is probably the first of the true Barberries to do so. The dark green, box-like foliage persists through all but the severest winters and the lovely orange-yellow flowers are produced, generally singly, from each tuft of leaves, followed by dark purple, globular fruits. Reproduction is by means of seed in February or cuttings in July. It grows about six feet in height and requires about the same space for spread. The two varieties *aureo-marginata* and *nana* have variegated foliage and are smaller and more compact respectively.

B. Darwinii is slightly taller, rising to 10 ft. and requires correspondingly more space. The foliage is small, dark green and holly-shaped and the flowers are the same colour as the last species but are generally to be found in clusters. Propagation is by cuttings in July and the flowering season slightly later than *B. buxifolia*.

B. linearifolia was only introduced in 1927. It has larger and brighter flowers than the last species and evergreen, entire, linear leaves. It is not a very robust species and prefers a moist, partially shaded site.

B. × *lologensis* is a hybrid of the last two species. It is an attractive evergreen shrub growing to no more than 3 ft. and bearing yellow flowers with reddish orange sepals in April and May. Propagation may be by means of cuttings in July or layers during the same month.

B. × *stenophylla* is a garden hybrid (*B. Darwinii* × *B. empetrifolia*) and is one of the most beautiful and most useful of the Barberries. During April and May the slender, interwoven branches become wreathed in Golden-yellow flowers, individually small but collectively breath-taking. The berries are black and farinous. There are many sub-species and varieties and all add their quota of beauty. These include 'Brilliant', *'coccineia'*, *'corallina'*, *'Irwinii'* and *'semperflorens'*, all of which grow about 8 ft. in height and require the same space for spread. Propagate by cuttings taken in August.

B. yunnanensis is a Chinese species growing to only 4 ft. in height. It is spherical in habit, with rather small leaves and pale yellow flowers borne in clusters and followed by brilliant red berries. Propagate by February sown seeds.

Camellia japonica was first introduced in 1739 and was originally cultivated as a greenhouse plant. They can however, be grown very successfully out of doors. The beautiful, smooth, green foliage is evergreen and the delicate blooms are borne in April and May. There are a number of varieties bearing flowers varying in colour from white, soft pink to deep rose and carmine, both single and double. They vary in height from 4 ft. to 15 ft. and are best propagated by leaf cuttings as described in the last chapter. There are other species including *C. cuspidata*, *C. reticulata* and *C. sasanqua* all of which grow to about 4 ft. in height and are worth considering. The last named flowers in January so should perhaps have been considered more correctly in Chapter VIII.

Chaenomeles $\times$ *superba* is one of the finest spring flowering shrubs in the garden. Growing to between 5 ft. and 8 ft. in height it bears its red flowers in April. Propagation is by means of layers or seed. There are many varieties to choose from, most of which have the characteristic red flowers, but some are paler in colour to almost white.

There is also *C. speciosa*, better known perhaps as *Pyrus japonica* of earlier days and its numerous varieties. Chaenomeles is, of course, a deciduous genus and is therefore extremely dull in winter. *Clematis montana* is a particularly useful and attractive deciduous climber, possessing three-parted leaves. The mass of clear white flowers appear during April and are reminiscent of wood anemones. They grow especially well on a limey building site soil, but should be planted with their roots in the shade. They grow comparatively quickly and are therefore very useful for covering new buildings or archways in a new garden. Propagation is difficult for the amateur, though is best attempted by means of layers. The variety 'Wilsonii' is fragrant and flowers in the autumn. *Cornus Nuttallii* is a tree rather similar to Dogwood which, in its native land grows to 75 ft. in height. In this country however, it seldom grows to more than 15 ft. and is therefore quite suitable for the small garden. The clematis-like flowers are yellowish when they first appear in April, later changing to white. They are actually formed from petal-like bracts surrounding the true flower which is an insignificant greenish button-like structure. Reproduce from seeds sown into pots and transplant only from pots, as they do not take kindly to disturbance.

Cytisus. The Broom family are all lovers of sunshine and this fact should be borne in mind when planting is carried out. Generally speaking plants growing on their own roots are best for acid and neutral soils but plants grafted on to Laburnum stocks are better for calcareous soils. Besides grafting, reproduction is carried out by means of stem cuttings.

C. albus growing to eight feet and bearing white

flowers on wand-like sprays above the grey-green foliage is a delightful shrub of garden origin.

C × praecox and its variety *'albus'* is a hybrid of *C. purgans* × *C. albus* and is known as the Warminster Broom. It is a gracefully habited, grey-green leaved shrub with arching sprays of sulphur-yellow flowers appearing in April.

C. purgans is one of the best known and most attractive species, with narrow leaves and masses of deep yellow flowers borne in the axils of the sturdy, upright sprays. Sometimes it will produce a second crop of flowers in the Autumn. This species only reaches 3 ft. in height.

C. scoparius is the common yellow Broom and is a magnificent plant which is worth its place in every garden. There are several varieties with flowers of various combinations including yellow and mahogany, brownish red and yellow, orange-yellow and crimson, yellow and buff. All grow to 6 ft. and require an area of 7 ft. in which to spread. Propagation of all species of Cytisus is by means of cuttings with a heel.

Daphne mezereum is a common cottage garden subject of great charm. The mauve flowers appear on the twiggy, bare stems in March and are delightfully fragrant. These are followed by red berries which are poisonous. Propagation is by means of seeds sown in February or cuttings in July. The species grows little more than 2 ft. in height and requires about the same space in which to spread. Any soil will prove adequate. There are three varieties of interest, those are *'alba'* with white flowers, *'grandiflora'* with larger flowers and *'autumnalis'* which flowers during the autumn.

Erica arborea is the Tree Heath which originated in the Mediterranean area and which grows from 6 ft. to 10 ft. in height, needing about the same area for spread. It possesses stout, hairy stems, smooth, greyish leaves arranged in threes and it bears sweetly fragrant, white flowers in large compound clusters during March and April. This species is evergreen and may be reproduced from seed sown in February. An acid soil is required as with all species of Heaths. Its variety *alpina* is slightly smaller and rather more hardy in habit.

Forsythia intermedia 'spectabilis' is to my mind the most lovely of the several species and varieties available and suitable for the small garden. The flowers appear in March and April and consist of dense clusters of golden yellow flowers. The shrubs of this species grow some 7 ft. in height and are easily propagated from July struck cuttings. Any type of soil will be satisfactory but an area some 7 ft. in diameter is desirable. Pruning if any, should be carried out directly after flowering, as the flowers are borne on the old wood. *F. suspensa* is slightly larger in size and bears pendulous flower. *F. giraldiana* is smaller and bears paler yellow flowers and *F. viridissima* has a greenish tinge in the otherwise characteristic yellow flowers.

Kerria japonica is an easy species to grow in any normal garden soil and it may be propagated easily by division in March. Originating, as the name tells us, from Japan, it has bright green, lanceolate, serrated leaves which, for their topmost lengths are wreathed with bright yellow, five-petalled flowers in April. The height and spread are from 4 ft. to 6 ft. There is also the variety *'pleniflora'*, which has double flowers appearing from spring to autumn.

Magnolia. There is a wide variety of Magnolias for the garden, many of which in their native habitat, grow immensely tall but which, under cultivation, maintain no more than reasonable proportions.

M. denudata, sometimes called *M. conspicua* grows to somewhere between 10 ft. and 20 ft. It prefers a sheltered position where it is not affected by morning sun. The snow-white flowers appear in March even on the smallest and youngest plants. Propagate in February by seed.

M. liliflora is probably the best variety of all for the small garden. It grows very slowly, ultimately reaching something less than 10 ft., has oval, long, green leaves, paler below, and flowers before the leaves are produced. The flowers, white inside and wine-red outside, appear in April. Propagation is by seed, layer or cuttings.

M. sargentiana is one of the larger species I recommend for small gardens, forming a graceful tree about 25 ft. high. The goblet-shaped flowers, white tinted with violet, are only borne on the mature plant. They appear in April. Propagate by seed. *M.* × *soulangiana* is a hybrid of *M. denudata* × *M. liliflora* which grows quickly to maturity. Flowers and leaves appear together in

April, white in colour and flushed purple outside. Its varieties *'alba'* and *'Alexandrina'* are also worth growing.

M. stellata is very slow-growing and covers itself, in March, before the leaves appear, with semi-double, white flowers. It seldom reaches more than 10 ft. in height and flowers very young. Propagate by seed, layers and cuttings.

Mahonia aquifolium, as is the case with all the other Magonias, is correctly a Berberis, but for convenience I have grouped them separately. This species, which is sometimes called the Oregon Grape is a fine plant for growing under trees. The evergreen, compound leaves are made up of from five to nine leaflets, each shaped like those of holly and they take on a purple tinge in winter. The bright yellow flowers are produced in crowded sprays from February onwards to the end of April. This species grows to 3 ft. in height but needs double that space for spread. Propagation is by February sown seeds or division of roots in October. *M. japonica* is another species of this group but with larger habit, both in growth and size of its bronzy foliage, than the last. The fragrant yellow flowers are borne in March. This species is reproduced by means of layers.

Osmanthus Delavayi is an evergreen shrub growing to 6 ft. in height and bearing its clusters of tubular, fragrant white flowers in April. Propagate by means of cuttings in July and August and plant in any soil.

O. serrulatus is a smaller growing plant with shiny, bright green leaves, minutely toothed and with similar flowers.

Paeonia moutan is a rigid branched shrub, sometimes called the Tree Paeony. It rarely exceeds 5 ft. in height, bears large leaves, sometimes up to 18 inches in length. The single varieties have from five to ten petals but the double varieties are fully double. The original colour of the species was rose purple, but all shades are available nowadays from white to crimson. The flowers begin to appear in April lasting until June. Propagation is carried out by means of layers in April.

Pieris floribunda is an exceptionally attractive evergreen shrub with dark green, pointed leaves and sprays of small, white, bell-shaped flowers appearing in March. Both height and spread of this species is about 5 ft. Propagate by cuttings in August and plant in an acid soil. *P. japonica* is another species of similar size but with rather more beautiful foliage.

Prunus is a vast species which embraces a number of popular garden trees such as Almond (*P. Amygdalus*), Cherry (*P. cerasus*), Cherry Laurel (*P. laurocerasus*), Apricot (*P. Armeniaca*), Bird Cherry (*P. Padus*), and Peach (*P. Persica*). Cultivation is greatly helped by the fact that they appear to grow well in almost any reasonably good soil. Propagation is by seed which is slow but accurate, or cuttings.

Rather than confuse the reader with a long list of species I give a few selections of the best.

P. Amygdalus is particularly suitable for an industrial area where the sulphurous atmosphere discourages both bull-finches and leaf-curl.

P. tangutica is perhaps a shade earlier than the last species flowering in March, but is more beautiful and more difficult to grow. It grows about 10 ft. in height.

P. tenella is the dwarf Almond only reaching 3 ft. in height. It is easy to reproduce by layers.

P. Persica the common Peach is a good strong growing plant for any garden. It does not however take kindly to being moved carelessly.

P. conradinae is the earliest flowering Cherry as

its fragrant white blossoms appear on the naked branches in February and sometimes even in January. Its variety *'semi-plena'* has semi-double, pink flowers.

P. subhirtella 'pendula' is the weeping cherry which can be a very beautiful tree, but which needs careful training in its early stages to produce the gracefully curved branches.

P. incisa is one of the most indispensable species of early cherries for the small garden.

Pyrus is another large group of trees and shrubs which include a number of excellent ornamental species. The list is large and once again I select a few of the better species. Both with the Prunus and Pyrus one is advised to visit a Nursery when the plants are in flower before making one's choice. Propagation is generally by means of grafting in March or budding in July.

P. aldenhamensis has exceptionally large, wine red flowers in April. The foliage is purple red. (12—30 ft.)

P. earlhamensis has bronze-green foliage and deep pink flowers in April, followed by large, apple-like, crimson fruits. (12—30 ft.)

P. florentina has grey-green foliage similar to the Hawthorn. During April it bears clusters of small white flowers followed by small red fruits spangled with brown patches. (8—12 ft.)

P. fusca is the Oregon Crab, with slender, reddish branches, dark-green foliage and brilliant flesh-pink flowers fading to white; followed by reddish-yellow fruits. (8—15 ft.)

P. orthocarpa is rather similar to the last species but the habit is smaller and the fruits are straight.

Rhododendron. There are so many species and hybrid varieties of this glorious family that it is difficult to advise the small gardener as to the best to buy, as it is so much a matter of personal choice and for this reason the best plan is to consult a local nurseryman's list. Rhododendrons can be moved easily at almost any size providing reasonable care is taken. They do however, insist on an acid soil. There is a wide range of colours available, from deep purple and deep ruby red, through all the pale colours to white. There are dwarf species and varieties no more than a few inches high and they can be obtained up to as high as 25 ft. to 30 ft. Propagation can be carried out in various ways, some species from seeds generally sown in February or March, others by means of cuttings, generally taken during July and finally some species are reproduced by means of layers.

Ribes sanguineum is the well-known Flowering Currant, noted for its hanging sprays of reddish-pink flowers in April. There are varieties '*albidum*' with white flowers tinged pink, *atrorubens* with crimson-red flowers and *splendens* with blood red flowers. All grow to between 4 ft. and 10 ft. and flower in March and April. Propagation is very easy and is carried out by means of cuttings struck in late summer.

Spiraea arguta is a hybrid of *S. Thunbergii* and *S. multiflora*. It is a neat shrub growing to about 4 ft. in height and bearing small heads of white flowers in wreath-like masses during April. Propagate by means of cuttings in July.

Viburnum Carlesii is a member of a large family which provides species to flower in practically every month of the year. This species has oval, felted leaves, dull green above and grey beneath, turning bright-red in autumn. The flowers, which appear in April, are pink in bud opening white. The whole shrub grows some 4 ft. in height and needs space for spread of 4 ft.

V. fragrans flowers from January to March and is slightly taller than the last species. Fragrant.

V. tinus flowers from November to April and is generally known as Laurestinus. The fragrant flowers are borne in flat clusters but are coloured the same as the last two species.

CHAPTER VI

Early Summer Species

May and June

WHEN THE lovely spring flowering species of trees and shrubs have finished their season of beauty the keen gardener will have alternative species which will provide colour for the next couple of months and so on throughout the year. Seasons are at best only arbitrary divisions and the times and length of flowering are governed far more closely by the weather conditions prevailing each year and many of the species discussed in the last chapter will be flowering during most of the month of May and possibly into June as well.

Abutilon vitifolium forms a tall shrub from 8 ft. to 12 ft. high. It possesses low-forking tree-like growth bearing large greyish, maple-like leaves and its transparent pale mauve flowers appear

61

in June. There is also *A. megapotamicum* with deep green, simple leaves with serrated margins. The pendant flowers are borne in the leaf axils from June onwards and consist of bright red calices, lemon-yellow petals and exserted, purple brown stamens. This species only grows to about 3 ft. in height.

Aesculus splendens is one of the shrubs belonging to the Horse Chestnut family. Sometimes called the Scarlet Buckeye this is the most delightful species of all. The eight-inch panicles of scarlet flowers appear in May. This plant is not particularly fussy over its treatment and requires only a normally good soil. Reproduction is by means of layers.

Bruckenthalia spiculifolia is a heather-like plant with dark needle-like evergreen foliage whitish beneath. The rose-pink heather-like flowers are loosely packed at the tips of the foliage and appear in June. This species only grows a foot tall.

Buddleia alternifolia rather resembles a weeping willow in habit and the sweet-smelling lilac flowers appear in June. This species grows to 8 ft. and requires a similar sized area in which to spread. Propagation is by seed or cuttings in

February and July respectively.

Caragana Boisii is a small shrub no more than 4 ft. tall with pinnate, multiple leaflets heavily spined with typical yellow pea flowers. There is also *C. chamlagu* with dark green leaves in two pairs and larger reddish yellow flowers. Seeds and July cuttings form the methods of reproduction. Both flower in May and require a slightly acid soil.

Ceanothus cyaneus is one of the hardiest evergreen species. The panicles of cornflower blue flowers which appear in May are among the largest of the flowering evergreens. It requires only normal soil and an area of 10 ft. for spread. It grows to 8 ft. in height and is reproduced by means of cuttings in July. There is also *C. dentatus* with small, notched evergreen leaves and deep blue flowers which is a shade larger than the last species. *C. Fendleri* is a dwarf (4 ft.), deciduous species with white or very pale blue flowers and small foliage.

Cercis siliquastrum is an attractive tree or shrub, attaining 10—15 ft. in height, with glaucous, round leaves, slightly flattened or pointed at the tips. The attractive, rosy-lilac, pea flowers are produced in clusters in May, before the leaves appear, at the joints of the old wood, often upon the mature branches or the trunk itself. Propagate by seed.

Chionanthus retusa is a handsome deciduous shrub growing to about 10 ft. high. The feathery masses of snow-white flowers appear in June. There is also *C. virginica* which is almost similar but with flowers that are slightly fragrant. Both species require a normal soil and are propagated by means of layers.

Choisya ternata is known as the Mexican Orange Flower and provides a roundish shrub about 8 ft. in height. The foliage is evergreen and glossy and the large clusters of fragrant, white flowers are borne in May though it has been known to throw an autumn crop of blossom. Propagate by cuttings in June.

Cistus. This genus provides a number of species very suitable for the small garden, varying in height from 2 ft. to 8 ft. None needs more than an average good soil but they are better if grown in a sheltered part of the garden.

C. albidus has lilac-pink flowers with a patch of yellow on each petal.

C. corbariensis bears red buds opening white

with yellow centres.

C. crispus, deep rose, *C. cyprius*, white, patched red. *C. ladaniferus*, white, patched chocolate, *C. Loretii*, white, patched scarlet, *C. salvifolius*, yellow, patched white and *C. Wintoniensis*, white, patched maroon. All the above species flower in May and June.

Convolvulus cneorum is a shining, silvery-leaved bush with narrow, elliptical leaves, which bears clusters of pink buds which open to typical, white, trumpet-shaped flowers in June. The height may be 3 ft. and it requires the same sized area for spread. Propagation is by means of cuttings struck during June.

Cornus kousa is a small bushy tree growing to 15 ft. in height. The flowers are insignificant but they are surrounded by four large creamy-white bracts in May. The foliage of this species is exceptionally beautiful before it falls in the autumn.

Coronilla emerus is a very fine and hardy shrub growing about 6 ft. high. The bright green pinnate leaves make a lovely setting for the yellow pea-like flowers which are borne in May and again in October. There is also *C. glauca* which is a slightly taller species with grey-green foliage.

The flowers are similar to the previous species but in sheltered positions they will continue from June until Christmas. Both species are propagated by means of cuttings taken in July.

Crataegus oxyacantha is more generally known as the May or Hawthorn and is one of the most beautiful of our native flowering trees. They do, however, prefer a calcareous soil. There are several varieties all of which bear flowers in some shade of pink or rose during May. *C. Lavallei* is a slightly larger species growing to about 20 ft. in height and bearing white flowers. Propagation is by means of seeds from the berries.

Cytisus. Besides the species referred to in the last chapter, there are certain later flowering species which fit in well to the May and June programme. The first of these is *C. Battandieri* which is an exceptionally beautiful, tall-growing variety with large silvery-grey leaves and white woolly stems which terminate with tightly packed spires of golden-yellow, sweetly scented flowers.

Some of the hybrids from *C. albus* × *C. scoparius* provide lovely varieties for the garden. These include 'Dorothy Walpole' with flowers deep pink and maroon, 'Enchantress', two shades of pink and 'Geoffrey Skipwith', rose-purple and cerise.

Another hybrid formed from crossing *C. andoinii* × *C. albus* provides us with 'Lord Lambourne', yellow, flushed pink and maroon and 'Lady Moore' yellow, flushed pink and orange.

Daphne is another genus which provides a wealth of colour for the May and June period in the garden. All are comparatively dwarf in size.
D. alpina is deciduous with grey-green leaves and clusters of fragrant white flowers.
D. Burkwoodii has pointed, bright green, ever-green leaves and bears fragrant, pale pink flowers. *D. cneorum* is another evergreen with rose-pink flowers. *D. collina* (evergreen), has rose-pink flowers and is lilac scented and *D. retusa* (evergreen), which looks like a miniature tree, bears clear white, fragrant, tubular shaped flowers. All are easy to reproduce either by means of cuttings taken in July or seeds sown in February.
Deutzia is another genus of very floriferous shrubs which flower during the early part of summer. They like a well drained but moist soil and may be propagated by means of cuttings,

67

seeds or division. The choice for tne smaller garden is wide and the following are suggested: *D. corymbosa* (4 ft.), white with yellow anthers; *D. kalmiaeflora* (3 ft.), pink; *D. longifolia* (8 ft.), rose pink, requires partial shade. *D. magnifica* (8 ft.), double white. *D. purpurascens* (6 ft.), white tinted crimson, requires a sheltered site.

Diervilla is better known to many people as Weigela. They are both useful and ornamental. The flowers, which are borne in the top-most axils of the previous year's wood, resemble those of the Foxglove. Most of the garden forms are hybrids and the best varieties include 'Abel Carriere', pale rose, 'Avantgarde', bright pink, 'Bouquet Rose', silver pink, 'La Perle', cream, 'Mont Blanc', white and 'Saturne', carmine. All of the above varieties grow to about 6 ft. in height and may be propagated by means of cuttings or division. *D. lonicera* i an American species growing to 4 ft. in height and bearing pale yellow flowers flushed with brown.

Dipelta floribunda is a species which is very similar to the Diervillas. The fragrant pink flowers with yellow throats are borne upon upright bushes which attain some 9 ft. in height. *D. ventricosa* is similar to the last species except that the throats are orange-coloured whereas *D. yunnanensis* is more dwarf in habit and bears white flowers flushed pink, with orange throats. All flower in May.

Erinacea pungens is a dwarf, spiny shrub which never attains more than a foot in height. It requires cool rooting conditions in a sunny, open site and without these conditions is a shy flowerer. The blue-grey, pea-like flowers appear in May. It is evergreen yet the foliage is inconspicuous. Propagate by means of cuttings in October.

Escallonia is another genus which possesses a relatively large number of species which flower within the period under discussion, and beyond it. All can be reproduced by means of July struck cuttings and many of them by seed as well. The height of the different species varies from 3 ft. to 12 ft. and the space required is generally the same as the height. For general purposes the hybrids are better than the species and 'Donard Beauty' (rose-red), 'Donard Brilliance' (crimson), 'Donard Gen' (pale pink) and 'Donard Seedling' (pale pink), are recommended. There is also 'Inveyana' for those who want a white variety. All are evergreen.

Exochorda is a useful genus for the small garden though there is comparatively little difference between the four species. Propagation is easy, offering, seeds, cuttings or division. There is: *E. Giraldii* (8 ft.), *E. Korolkowii* (8 ft.), *E. macrantha* (9 ft.) and *E. racemosa* (10 ft.). All bear white flowers in May.

Fabiana imbricata is a small, heath-like shrub growing about 5 ft. in height. The small trumpet-like flowers commence in May and usually last until August. There is also its variety *'violacea'* with greyish-blue flowers. Propagation is by means of cuttings in July.

Fremontia californica is an ideal subject for those who possess a soil of poor quality. Though not entirely evergreen many of the leaves remain on the plant throughout the winter. It requires shelter and with the most suitable conditions will produce an abundance of yellow flowers from May onwards throughout the summer. It will grow to 10 ft. in height and should be given the same sized space for spread.

Fuchsia magellanica is the parent of most garden fuchsias. Its long pendulous flowers, made up of scarlet calyx and purple corolla appear in June

70

and last until October. It will grow to 6 ft. in height in sheltered places in this country and is particularly common in the South Western counties. There is also its variety *'alba'* with very pale flowers, which is stronger in habit than the parent plant. There are other varieties available but *'Riccartonii'* is perhaps the best in every way.

Halesia carolina, or the Snowdrop Tree, will flourish in a soil that is without lime. It is a beautiful plant with spreading habit growing to some 15 ft. in height. The drooping sprays of white, snowdrop-like flowers appear in May and June. Propagation is best carried out by means of layers in April.

Halimiocistus Sahucii is a dwarf shrub which produces a profusion of white, buttercup-like flowers at the end of June. Evergreen by nature it grows a foot high. Propagation is by means of cuttings in August.

Halimodendron argenteum is a handsome shrub growing to 6 ft. in height with grey foliage and producing small, pinkish pea flowers in June. Propagate from seeds in February. A good plant for poor soils.

Jasminum officinale is one of the ever popular species of Jasmine which bears its fragrant white flowers in June and onwards. This species, which grows to 10 ft. in height, is at its best as a climber against the house or over an archway. Another useful summer species is *J. revolutum* with its dark green leaves and large, sweetly scented, yellow flowers which are borne in attractive sprays. Both these two species are deciduous and are reproduced from August struck cuttings.

Kalmia angustifolia is a compact and very neat shrub with dull evergreen leaves, producing, at the upper part of the previous year's growth, rosy-red umbrella shaped flowers with projecting stamens. There is also *K. latifolia* which is an outstanding species bearing deep rose, saucer-shaped flowers. Both species attain some 3 ft. in height and require a sandy soil.

Kolkwitzia amabilis is a pretty and easily grown shrub growing from 3 ft. to 6 ft. in height. The foliage is hairy, long pointed and deciduous while the Weigela-like flowers are bright pink with yellow throats. Propagate from June struck cuttings.

Laburnum. There is little difference between the species of this glorious early summer tree except in shape and colour of foliage. The typical long sprays of bright yellow flowers appear in May and June. *L. Vosii* and *L. Watereri* are the two best garden hybrids. Heights vary between 10 ft. and 30 ft. and they should be allowed 15 ft. in which to spread. These two species are reproduced by grafting.

Leptospermum is an ideal subject for the South and West of these islands and they will tolerate practically any type of soil providing there is an absence of lime. The species are propagated by seed and the hybrids by cuttings. *L. baccatum* (6 ft.), white flowers flushed pink, *L. pubescens* (6 ft.), white and its variety *'Chapmanii'* (6 ft.), bright pink.

Lonicera Brownii is a hybrid from *L. Sempe-ruirens* × *L. hirsuta*, commonly known as Scarlet Trumpet Honeysuckle. It is a glorious climber for a partially shaded site. The yellow, tubular flowers with their orange-scarlet exterior decoration, appear from June to September. *L. nitida* is the well-known hedging shrub but used as a single subject in a bed of flowering shrubs it will help to fill up the gaps. In addition, it bears small, sweetly scented white flowers in May, which are followed by purple violet berries. Grown thus it should not be trimmed as is necessary with plants used in hedges. Evergreen in habit it will grow to 8 ft. and may be reproduced by means of cuttings in July.

Lupinus arboreus is the well known tree Lupin which has the advantage of being a rapid grower, though it is not long-lived. Propagation is easy from seeds which are generously produced. The sulphur-yellow flowers are borne in cylindrical spires in June. This species is evergreen and attains as much as 6 ft. in height. Its variety 'Snow Queen' bears white flowers.

Magnolia acuminata 'cordata' is an early summer flowering deciduous species of that famous genus, which only grows to 10 ft. in height. The canary coloured flowers and foliage are both fragrant. There is also *M. parviflora* which attains no more than 3 ft. The large, white flowers with their pink sepals are as sweetly scented as its brethren and it is therefore particularly useful for the small garden.

Menziesia purpurea is a delightful and rather rare shrub rather similar to Erica, which grows to

5 ft. The oval, green leaves are blue-grey beneath and deciduous. The sprays of nodding, wine-red flowers are displayed in May and June. The foliage is particularly beautiful during the autumn. Propagate by means of June struck cuttings.

Philadelphus or the Mock Orange has several useful species which are exceptionally easy to cultivate as they will thrive in any soil. Propagation is generally by means of July struck cuttings. The commonest varieties are a group of hybrids which will grow up to 8 ft. and which require the same area for spread. There are single and double varieties, some of which are fragrant. The flowers are generally white but in some cases tinted with pink or mauve. Some of the best varieties include 'Argentine' (single), 'Belle Etoile' (single), 'Bouquet Blanche' (double), 'Manteau d'Hermione' (double, dwarf), 'Virginale' (double) and 'Voie Lactée' (single).

Ptelea trifoliata, the hop Tree, is useful for those wishing for something unusual. It is a slowish grower, seldom reaching more than 20 ft. in height. The greenish-white flowers are fragrant and appear in June. Propagate by seed in October.

Rhododendron. There are many species and hybrids of this wonderful genus which will not commence flowering until May and June and the advice I gave in the last chapter applies equally for this season. Decide on the colours required, time of flowering and approximate size and then consult a specialist who will advise the most suitable species or varieties to grow. Otherwise, with a list of varieties, I have frequently found that one makes elaborate plans and either the nurseryman will never have heard of them or they will not be available and one will have to start all over again.

Robinia hispida is an easy subject to grow. The hanging Wisteria-like sprays of pale pink flowers are freely produced during May and June. A deciduous species, it will grow some 5 ft. in height and may be propagated by means of seeds sown in October. There is also *R. Kelseyi* which is double the size of the last species and which is also propagated by seeds, but this time from a February sowing.

Roses. There are so many different types of rose and so many hundreds of varieties that it would be ludicrous in a book of this size to attempt to advise the reader, as everyone has his or her own favourite in type and colour. The same remarks apply here as for Rhododendron and one should visit the local nursery to see what is available as many nurseries will only grow the more common varieties, such as Peace, The Doctor, Speks Yellow, Frau Karl Druschky, Ena Harkness, President Hoover, and many, many others.

Solanum crispum is a fine, partially climbing shrub, sometimes evergreen, with large open clusters of bluish-yellow flowers with yellow eyes. Best grown in the protection of a wall it provides a most attractive picture during the summer and early autumn. Growing to 10 ft. in height it is partially evergreen and may be reproduced either by seeds sown in February or July struck cuttings.

Sophora tetraptera is a small tree of 10 ft. or so with bright evergreen leaves and sprays of tubular, golden-yellow flowers hanging in some profusion. There is also *S. viciifolia* which is a smaller species of deciduous habit. The flowers are violet-blue and white. Propagate both by means of July struck cuttings.

Spiraea is another genus which provides species to flower at various times of the year. For the season discussed in this chapter there is *S. bella* which bears small, compound clusters of bright pink flowers, neatly distributed on rounded shrubs which seldom attain more than 3 ft. in height. *S. bracteata* is a slightly taller species bearing large composite groups of clear white flowers. *S. canescens* is slightly larger still and bears creamy white flowers.

Staphylea colchica is a 6 ft. deciduous shrub of erect growth, bearing clusters of white flowers in May. The flowers are followed by bladder-like fruits. There is also *S. holocarpa 'rosea'* which is just as beautiful and has pink flowers.

Styrax americana is suited to the milder parts of the country. It is rather similar to the 'Snowdrop Tree' and the drooping white flowers are borne on the 8 ft. shrub in June. Propagate by July struck cuttings.

Syringa vulgaris is in my opinion one of the most beautiful of our garden shrubs. There are numerous varieties and hybrids covering a range of colours from deep purple, through the mauves and pinks to white. In size they will vary from 3 ft. to 15 ft. There are several species, all of which are useful, though less commonly seen in this country.

Tricuspidaria lanceolata is an evergreen shrub, hardy only in the South and West, which has deep-green, elliptical, pointed leaves and which bears its quaint hanging flowers of sealing-wax red on long red stems in May and onwards. Its height is about 8 or 9 ft. Propagate by July struck cuttings.

Viburnum is a genus which possesses a number of species which show their flowers in the months of May and June. For the small garden however I do not recommend them as being of sufficient merit to compete with other summer flowering species. On the other hand, the winter flowering species are ideal to provide a measure of winter blossom. For that reason I shall not use up more space by describing summer flowering species of this genus.

Wisteria sinensis is the outstanding species of a lovely genus though it must be used in a position where it can climb to an indefinite distance, such as up the side of a house or over a pergola. The foot long sprays of large, mauve, scented flowers appear in May and June. Propagation is by means of layers taken in May or cuttings in August.

Zenobia pulverulenta is a small shrub growing to 3 ft. in height bearing white, bell-shaped flowers. It requires an acid soil and partial shade.

CHAPTER VII

Late Summer Species

July and August

THE MONTHS of July and August see the heat of summer and with it there are a number of very lovely flowering shrubs. On the other hand, it is at this season that the effects of lime-free or acid-free soils may be noticed more than at other times, particularly as these shortages may rule out the chance of growing some of the choicer subjects. Similarly, those people resident in the North may be more restricted by the normally cooler climate than their fellow countrymen living in the South.

The following is a selection of flowering trees and shrubs suitable for the late summer months.

Abelia is a small group of shrubs, consisting of both evergreen and deciduous species. First of all there is *A. chinensis* growing to 3 ft. which makes a round shrub with reddish branches and light green leaves. The white flowers are sweetly scented and are surrounded by a red calyx. Deciduous. There is also *A. floribunda* an evergreen species growing to 6 to 8 ft. The flowers, borne in twos or threes are rose purple. *A. grandiflora* is similar to but larger than *A. chinensis*. Finally *A. Schumannii* is another small deciduous shrub with rose-coloured flowers and foliage that becomes flushed with red. All may be propagated by July struck cuttings.

Begonia capreolata is an attractive semi-evergreen climber with orange-red funnel-shaped flowers and deep-green, heart-shaped leaves. This species will climb to 20 ft. and may be propagated from seeds sown in March.

Berberidopsis corallina is an evergreen climber with dark green, heart-shaped leaves, in the upper axils of which appear the deep red, pendant flowers. This too is evergreen and needs the protection of a wall.

Buddleia. Though one species of this well-known genus was mentioned in the last chapter, this is the season when most of its species will flower. First there is *B. albiflora*, a strong growing (10 ft.)

variety, with scented, lilac flowers, each with an orange centre. *B. auriculata* is almost evergreen and needs the protection of a South wall. The flowers are cream with yellow centres. *B. Fallowiana 'alba'* is a dwarf species with white, somewhat furry flowers. *B. variabilis* grows to 15 ft. and, according to the variety, will produce crowded, terminal sprays of purple to pink flowers. All species may be propagated from July struck cuttings.

Calluna vulgaris is very similar to the Erica and is a shrub which favours northern England and Scotland. Growing generally to some 2 ft. in height, it is evergreen and is propagated from cuttings in May. There is a wide selection of varieties, including 'alba' white, 'Alpworth' carmine, *'argentea'* purple, 'C. H. Beale', double pink, *'coccinea'* crimson, *'hypnoides'* purple, and *'pygmaea'* purple and very dwarf.

Caryopteris $\times$ *clandonensis* is a hybrid from *C. Mastacanthus* $\times$ *C. mongholica* and makes a fine shrub, 6 ft. high. The foliage is greenish-grey and the flowers deep lavender blue. *C. Mastacanthus* is more woody than the last species and the leaves are scented. All are propagated from cuttings in May and need a normal soil.

Ceanothus Burkwoodii is a hybrid from *C. floribundas* × *C. hybridus indigo* and is a later flowering species than those referred to in the last chapter. It grows to 9 ft., is evergreen in habit and throws dense sprays of bright blue flowers which appear in July and last until October. *C. hybridus* is the name given to many varieties which have formally been named under *C. Delilianus* and *C. pallidus*. These include 'Albert Pittet' bright pink, 'Ceres' mauve-pink, 'Charles Detriche' dark blue, 'Gloire de Versailles' powder blue and 'Perle Rose' carmine.

Ceratostigma Willmottianum is a nice 2 ft. deciduous shrub with bright blue flowers appearing in August. It needs protection from East and North winds and pays for a fairly rich and slightly acid soil. Propagate by means of cuttings in July.

Clematis Jackmanii is the name given to the most popular group of hybrids. There are many varieties covering a wide range of colours. These are deciduous climbers which must be provided with support. Propagation is by means of cuttings struck in July. A few selections include the following, 'Alexandra' pale reddish-violet, 'Gipsy Queen' deep purple, *'alba'* white, *'rubra'* red. 'Mrs. Cholmondeley' pale blue, 'Perle d'Azure' bright blue and 'Rubella' deep claret. All will flower during the period May to October. There are also the hybrids from *C. lanuginosa.* These are very similar to the previous group and the following varieties are suggested: 'Beauty of Worcester' violet-blue (double and single on the same plant), 'Blue Gem' sky-blue, 'Crimson King' rose, 'Fairy Queen' flesh with pink bars, and 'Lord Neville' dark plum.

Clerodendron is a group of small trees and shrubs flowering in July and August. All grow about 9 ft. in height and can be propagated from root cuttings taken in April.

C. Bungei bears rounded heads of tightly packed, rosey-red, fragrant flowers.

C. Fargesii bears small white, star-shaped flowers which are also fragrant. These are followed by pale blue berries. There is also *C. trichotomum* which bears white flowers set in maroon calyces, followed by bright blue berries.

Clethra is another group of small trees and shrubs suitable for this period. All require a lime-free soil. *C. alnifolia* is the 'Sweet Pepper' and grows to 8 ft. It bears small, sweetly scented white flowers. Deciduous. *C. arborea* is called the Lily of the Valley Tree and grows up to 20 ft. It is evergreen and requires shelter even in the south-western counties to which it is restricted. *C. Delavayi* is somewhat similar to the last species except that it is deciduous, and requires similar conditions. *C. tomentosa* is more grey in its early life than *C. alnifolia* but otherwise it is very similar. Propagate from July cuttings.

Daboecia is a two-specied genus of dwarf shrubs which 'insist' on a lime-free soil. *D. azorica* has small, hairy, bronze-green leaves, and has ample oval bells of bright crimson on reddish stems. *D. cantabrica* bears rounded, oval flowers of rose-purple. There are also its varieties *'alba'* white, *'bicolour'* white with red markings, *'globosa'* pale purple and *'purpurea'* crimson-purple. All grow to about 1 ft. in height and can be propagated by cuttings in June and July.

Desfontainea spinosa is an unusual shrub which will grow to 8 ft. in a sheltered, shady and rather moist site. Its foliage is similar to a light green holly but it bears tubular, scarlet flowers tipped with yellow, from July to October. Propagation may be carried out from seeds sown in March or cuttings in July. In either case moist conditions must prevail.

Erica. A vast number of species, hybrids and varieties flower during the period under review. All need an acid soil and are propagated by summer struck cuttings. Beyond this I must refer readers to a specialist grower's catalogue, as the combination of sizes, colours and forms available would take far too much space in a book of this size which must cover so much ground.

Eucryphia cordifolia is the most useful species of this genus for the small garden. It is also, unfortunately, the most tender, but it repays every bit of the care and attention it demands. The heart-shaped, evergreen leaves are dull but are produced on downy branches. The clear white flowers, which appear in August, have bright terra cotta anthers. Propagate by seed in February.

Fatsia japonica is more generally known as *Arabia japonica.* It forms an attractive, evergreen shrub which bears white flowers in large panicles. It will grow to about 8 ft. in height and does best if given partial shade. Propagation is by means of cuttings struck in August.

Feijoa Sellowiana is another single species worth a place in a garden with a calcareous soil. It is propagated by July cuttings. Growing some 8 ft. in height it has evergreen leaves which are deep green above and white below and its large white flowers with red stamens appear in August.

Fuchsia magellanica and its varieties are the best of the genus for garden use. Of the varieties, *Riccartonii* is probably the best known. From July to September the 5 ft. shrub will be covered with a mass of its slender purple and scarlet flowers. Propagate by means of cuttings at any time from June to October.

Genista aethnensis is a fast growing, rush-like deciduous shrub with inconspicuous leaves. The yellow pea-like flowers appear at the tops of the slender stems in July and August.

Hibiscus syriacus is a deciduous shrub rising sometimes to 9 to 10 ft. Once established, even the most brutal pruning will not deter it. Propagation is by means of July struck cuttings. Of the many varieties the following are recommended: 'Admiral Dewey' double white, *'amplissimus'* double rosy purple, *'coelestis'* single blue, *'coelestis plenus'* double blue, *'monstrosus'* single white, *'roseus plenus'* double pink and *'speciosus'* double peach.

Hoheria lyallii is a beautiful, deciduous shrub growing up to 10 or 12 ft. The leaves are glaucous green and the white flowers resemble those of the cherry. Propagate by June struck cuttings.

Hydrangea paniculata is one of the species suitable for the garden. It has large green leaves and bears large white clusters of flowers, the sterile outer florets fading to pink with age. There is also *H. villosa* which has lance-shaped leaves, green above and grey below, and the central zone of small pale blue flowers is ringed and dotted with large, lavender-blue, sterile flowers. Both these species grow to 6 ft. and are propagated by means of July struck cuttings.

Hypericum is another genus with a fairly large number of July flowering species. Most are dwarf and the predominant colour for the flowers is yellow. Some are evergreen and some deciduous, so the choice is fairly wide. Propagation is by seed or cuttings. The following are recommended: *H. aureum*, 4 ft., fragrant. *H. Buckleyi*, 1 ft.

H. coris, 2/3 ft. (Best on a really poor soil). *H. Hookerianum*, 4 ft. *H. patulum* 'Forrestii', 3 ft. The foliage of this variety changes from bright red to green and back again to orange and crimson. *H. Rodgersii*, 10 ft. and *H. uralum*, 2 ft., but somewhat pendant and lax in growth.

Indigofera is a genus of deciduous shrubs, varying in height from 1 ft. to 6 ft. All are easy to propagate from seeds or cuttings. *I. decora* has reddish-brown stems and bears long sprays of pink pea-like flowers. It also has a variety *'alba'* with white flowers. Both are 1 ft. high. *I. pendula* is a spreading shrub with lacey branches and bearing drooping sprays of rosy-purple flowers. There are other species available, but the above two are recommended.

Koelreuteria paniculata is a very handsome shrub or small tree known sometimes as the Golden Rain Tree. In favoured districts it will attain as much as 30 ft. in height and it is easy to propagate from cuttings in August. The deep yellow flowers are borne in pyramidal panicles.

Lavandula. The Lavenders are delightful shrubs

which unite fragrance with silver grey and purple in their colouring. All the species are very similar, varying slightly in size and form. *L. dentata,* 3 ft., *L. lanata,* 1½ ft., *L. spica,* 3 ft. and its variety *'alba'* white flowered. *L. Stoechas,* 1 ft. has the deepest coloured flowers of all, and *L. vera,* 3 ft.

Lespedeza bicolor is a shrub is a shrub much resembling Indigofera and its cultivation is similar to members of that genus. It grows to 6 ft. in height and bears hanging sprays of bright purple pea flowers. There is also *L. formosum,* which is slightly smaller in habit bearing sprays of rose-purple flowers sometimes exceeding 2 ft. in length. Both species are deciduous and can be propagated by seeds sown during February.

Mutisia is a group of evergreen climbers with very large daisy-like flowers. An essential feature in their cultivation is to ensure that their roots cannot be dried out by direct sunshine, nor frozen during the winter. Propagate by suckers. *M. decurrens* has gazaria-shaped flowers of an orange vermilion colour with yellow disc-florets. *M. ilicifolia* has pink flowers or pale mauve flowers with yellow centres and *M. retusa* is a slightly better form of the last species, being hardier.

Nandina domestica is an 8 ft. shrub with a particularly graceful appearance, erect in growth and bearing evergreen foliage with attractive spring and autumn tones. The individual white flowers are small but are impressive in the mass and in favoured places are followed by coral red fruits. Propagate from seed.

Passiflora caerulea is the so-called Blue Passion Flower, the flowers of which may vary from 3 to 11 inches in diameter. A climber reaching up to 25 ft. it is best suited to a sheltered, sunny wall where its greyish-green palmate leaves will persist. Propagate from seeds or cuttings.

Perovskia atriplicifolia is a useful shrub, growing to about 4 ft., which will do well in any reasonably good garden soil. The greenish-grey foliage is deciduous and the violet blue flowers, somewhat similar to catmint, appear in August. Propagation is easy from suckers or cuttings.

Polygonum baldschuanicum is a rampant climber with green heart-shaped leaves and very large, drooping sprays of creamy white flowers produced with great freedom in August.

Propagate by means of cuttings.

Potentilla fruticosa is an upright shrub growing to 4 ft. The bright yellow flowers are produced in many small sprays throughout the summer. There are several varieties most of which are similar, though 'Vietchii' has white flowers and 'Vilmoriniana' has cream flowers. Propagate by means of cuttings in August.

Romneya is the Californian Tree Poppy. Both species grow some 4 ft. high and once established will spread rapidly. Propagation is by means of root cuttings. Both species *R. Coulteri* and *R. trichocalyx* are similar, bearing white, fragrant, poppy type flowers in July and August.

Senecio compactua, as the name implies is a compact, 2 ft. shrub with neat, silvery, serrated, evergreen leaves and heads of yellow daisy-type flowers. They grow in any good soil and propagate easily from cuttings.

Spartium junceum is the well-known Spanish Broom, a magnificent shrub of erect habit bearing clusters of yellow, fragrant, pea-like flowers in July and August. Propagate from seed in February.

Spiraea Aitchisonii forms a nice, 10 ft., well balanced shrub bearing long sprays of fluffy white flowers. The foliage is deciduous. Propagate from July cuttings. There is also *S. arborea* which is similar but the flowers are cream coloured, and *S. Douglasii* which is less tall and bears rose-pink flowers.

Stewartia is a small group of shrubs which insist on a lime-free soil. The flowers resemble those of the Camellia. Propagation is best carried out by means of layers in July, but cuttings can be taken during the same month. There is *S. koreana* (15 ft.) which has white flowers, *S. pentagyna* (9 ft.) with creamy white flowers centred by clusters of yellow stamens, and its variety 'grandiflora' which has fringed flowers and purple stamens, and *S. sinensis* (15 ft.) in which the flowers are clear white with golden stamens.

Tamarix is a group of graceful shrubs of varying heights which will do particularly well in coastal districts. They are freely propagated from cuttings in October. There is *T. anglica* (4 ft.), evergreen, bearing white flowers tinged with pink. *T. hispida* (3 ft.), deciduous, with pink flowers, and *T. pentandra* which is deciduous and grows to 12 ft. bearing pink flowers.

Trachelospermum asiaticum is a climber which needs the shelter of a south wall. The leaves are similar to those of the Periwinkle and the flowers are deep cream and sweetly scented, with yellow eyes. An acid soil is required. Propagate from cuttings in July.

Ulex nanus is a small evergreen shrub which seldom reaches more than 15 inches and which bears a mass of yellow flowers in the late summer.

Yucca is a small group of evergreen shrubs with stiff sword-like leaves and erect spikes of lily-like flowers. Propagation is easy from seed sown in October. This group is excellent in town conditions. *Y. filamentosa* (3 ft.) with deep cream flowers, *Y. glauca* (4 ft.) with greenish-yellow flowers, *Y. gloriosa* (8 ft.) creamy-white and *Y. recurvifolia* which is similar to the last species.

CHAPTER VIII

Autumn and Winter Species

September to January

NOW that the three best flowering periods of the year are past; namely spring, early summer and late summer, it is harder to find flowering shrubs and trees to provide gaiety and beauty during the autumn and winter.

Many of the species recommended for the last period (*see* Chapter VII), will carry on into September and even October, and a fairly large proportion of the early flowering species will provide a measure of beauty in the form of fruits and berries.

Let us now turn to the actual flowering species for this period and see what can be found.

Arbutus unedo is a small tree reaching about 15 ft. at maturity. With evergreen foliage it bears clusters of small, pinkish flowers followed by

96

round, hanging, orange fruits which ripen when the next year's flowers are produced. Preferring an acid soil it may be propagated by seeds sown in February (October to December).

Artemesia tridenata is a pleasant aromatic shrub growing to 8 ft. in height bearing silver-grey, evergreen leaves and small yellow flowers (October).

Clematis balearica has dark green, evergreen foliage which turns bronze in winter when the greenish-yellow flowers, spotted with purple are produced — (September to March). Somewhat similar is *C. cirrhosa* growing only to 8 ft. and with yellowish-white flowers — (January to March). There is also *C. paniculata* which is a vigorous climber bearing small, fragrant white flowers (September to October).

Colletia armata is a spined shrub growing to 8 ft. in height and bearing hawthorn scented flowers similar to, but smaller than, those of the Lily-of-the-valley (October).

Elaeagnus macrophylla is a pretty 8 ft. shrub, rounded in habit, with grey-green leaves bearing silvery Fuchsia-like flowers followed by red fruits

(October to November).

Elsholtzia Stauntonii is a lax shrub of rather untidy habit with leaves which smell strongly of mint when crushed. The flower spikes are woolly, dense and one-sided and bear lilac-purple flowers at the ends of the branches (September — October).

Erica carnea only grows to a foot in height but it possesses a wide range of winter flowering varieties with colours ranging from white to deep pink. Propagation is by means of cuttings struck in June. Of the varieties the following are particularly recommended, *'atroruba'* deep crimson, 'Cecilia N. Beale' white, 'King George' deep pink, 'Mrs. Doncaster' bright pink, 'Queen of Spain' pale pink, *'Vivelli'* crimson-carmine and 'Winter Beauty' very deep pink. All do well in any normal garden soil (December to March). There is also *E.* × *Darleyensis* 2 ft., dull pink (November to April).

Eucryphia cordifolia is a beautiful 10 ft. shrub or small tree which demands shelter and care and which pays handsome dividends for the attention bestowed upon it. The evergreen, heartshaped leaves are borne on downy branches and the clear white flowers have terra cotta anthers. Propagate from seed in February (September to October). *Eupatorium micranthum* is a quick growing shrub with oblong leaves and flat heads of fragrant white flowers (September to November).

Hamamelis is a group of winter flowering deciduous shrubs of various heights. Propagation should be carried out from seeds in February. There is *H. japonica*, pale yellow 10 ft. (January to February), and its varieties *'arborea'* yellow touched claret at the base (December to March), *H. mollis* yellow, 7 ft. (December to February), *H. vernalis* which has bright yellow autumnal foliage and fragrant red flowers, 6 ft. (January to February) and *H. virginiana* yellow, 8 ft. (September to November).

Jasminum nudiflorum is without doubt the best known and most loved species of its genus. The green stems bearing bright yellow flowers during the winter, before the arrival of the foliage, makes it an excellent plant to climb over a porchway. Propagate from cuttings in August. Any good soil is suitable (November to February).

Lithospermum rosmarinifolium is a rounded 1 ft.

99

shrub with hard woody stems, narrow green leaves and very large flowers of intense blue. It requires a slightly acid soil and can be propagated from cuttings in March (January to February).

Nuttallia cerasiformis is an easily grown 8 ft. shrub which bears drooping sprays of almond scented, greenish white flowers before the onset of the foliage. These are followed by purple fruits. Division is the best method of propagation, but cuttings can be struck in July (January to March).

Sarcococca Hookeriana is an upright, evergreen shrub of loose growth, reaching 3 ft. in height which bears sweetly scented white flowers, which are followed by blue-black berries (January to March).

Viburnum tinus, the well-known Laurustinus, is an evergreen shrub growing to about 8 ft. and producing flat clusters of pink buds opening to fragrant white flowers during the winter and early spring (November to April).

CHAPTER IX

Hedges

IN THE days of my grandfather there were few, if any, hedges made up exclusively of flowering shrubs. In those days the Yew hedge provided the hallmark of respectability. Next I suppose came the Privet, sometimes combined with the Quick-thorn to expedite growth. I suppose the Privet hedge is still as popular today as then, but largely, I think, because the number of gardens requiring a hedge have more than trebled. Lonicera, Laurel, Beech and Hornbeam, all make useful hedging subjects, as do Box, Holly and Cupressus Lawsoniana, but this book is chiefly concerned with flowering trees and shrubs and consequently it is a hedge made of this type of material that I want to consider now.

Flowering hedges are comparatively little used in this country for some unaccountable reason, except in Devon and Cornwall. In Germany however, and parts of France they are the rule rather than the exception. Both evergreen and deciduous subjects are used, depending upon the actual location; plants are selected for their capacity for flowering or for bearing berries, or both.

Generally speaking one must sacrifice formality to gain beauty as it is not so easy to keep many of the flowering shrubs closely pruned and still expect them to bear a profusion of flowers, though it can be done if suitable subjects are chosen. However, let us discuss the plants we use later.

In preparing for a hedge the soil should be prepared every bit as carefully as it was for the shrub and tree borders. First, it should be double dug and enriched with some well rotted compost and a dressing of bone meal. This should be done two or three weeks before planting is carried out.

Deciduous hedges can be planted either in early spring or autumn, but a mild spell of weather should be taken advantage of. Evergreens are generally planted in late spring or the autumn. After planting is completed the plants should be cut back one-third to induce bushy growth. Planting distances will depend on the genera used, but will be much closer than was the case when the same species are used as shrubs, generally speaking 1½ to 2 ft. apart will be correct. Firm planting is essential in every case and during a hot spell after planting an adequate supply of water must be given.

Let us turn now to the most suitable genera and species of flowering shrubs for the hedge.

Berberis provides us with three species *B. darwinii, B. stenophylla* and *B. atrocarpa,* which make a hedge some 6 to 8 ft. tall bearing arching sprays of yellow flowers in spring, followed by berries in the autumn.

Rhododendron myrtifolium and *R.* × *praecox* make excellent, small, compact hedges and the common Rhododendron will provide a larger and more informal type. All will provide a wealth of bloom during May and June with colours according to variety.

Ribes sanguineum, the Flowering Currant, makes a sparkling hedge of red or crimson for several weeks during the spring.

Forsythia ovata is the best species of this lovely genus for hedging purposes and has the advantage that it can be pruned fairly well to shape each year.

Fuchsia magellanica 'Riccartonii' with its glorious display of pendant carmine and purple flowers during late summer is another plant which cari be kept more or less in order for hedge purposes.

Syringa vulgaris the Common Lilac, provides a wealth of beauty in May and can be adapted well for the hedge. In Germany one frequently sees a combination of two or more of the last three species I have given used in hedges, thus giving a flowering season in February and March, late April to early June and again from July to August.

Spiraea argenta, the White Bridal Wreath and *S. bullata* with its red flowers, both flowering during the summer make useful plants. There is also *S. × Van Houttei* with white flowers in the spring which is a useful subject on poor soils.

Genista hispanica, the Spanish Gorse, makes a fine medium sized hedge and is covered with a mass of golden yellow flowers throughout May and June.

Erica meditteranea 'W. T. Rackliff' makes a useful low hedge and is covered with its characteristic white flowers from March until May.

Lavender is another well-known subject for a low hedge providing both beauty of foliage and scent.

Rosemarinus officinalis, the Rosemary, is clustered with its lavender blue flowers in April and May. Some people are shy of having Rosemary in the garden due to the old fashioned saying that 'If Rosemary flowers in your garden Ma wears the pants!'

Santolina chamaecyparissus is an aromatic shrub which is admirably suited to form a low hedge bearing yellow buttons from June till August. There are also *S. pinnata* and *S. viridis* both of which are equally suitable though slightly smaller and both of which produce very pale yellow flowers in July.

Hyssopus officinalis will form a 2 ft. hedge, covered from August to September with violet blue flowers. The varieties *'albus'*, white and *'roseus'* pink are equally suitable. There is also

H. aristatus which grows slightly taller and bears purple flowers.

Viburnum tinus, the Laurustinus, discussed earlier in this book, is another useful evergreen plant. It has the advantage too of flowering during the winter. A hedge of this material will naturally be of looser texture than any of the species referred to above.

Caragana arborescens has attractive apple green foliage and yellow, pea-like flowers in May. There is also *C. chamlagu* which bears orange flowers at the same time. Both make a hedge 4 ft. high.

Escallonia, with its flowers in various shades of red and pink, also white, will make another attractive informal hedge, flowering during the summer. This too is evergreen.

Ceanothus has several species and varieties suitable for informal hedging and the colours may range from pink to blue.

Chaenomeles Japonica (perhaps better known as Cydonia) makes a nice bushy hedge either tall or medium in size. This is another species used extensively in Germany, where the orange-scarlet, crimson, rose or white flowers are no uncommon sight from March until May.

Hydrangea paniculata is used by some people for hedge work. Personally I think it is the wrong use for the Hydrangea and would never consider its use. If used it will flower from July to September.

Cotoneaster simonsii is a grand hedge shrub with foliage which persists through all but the severest winters and is prettily tinted. These are accompanied for a long period by groups of orange-scarlet berries.

Osmanthus aquifolium provides a mass of small, white and exceptionally fragrant flowers during September and October. This species requires to be used in a sheltered position.

Pyracantha Rogersiana bears a mass of snow white flowers in June which are followed by orange berries.

Olearia haastii will make a 3 ft. hedge bearing a

mass of small, hawthorn scented, white daisy flowers in July and August. Another of the same genus is *O. macrodonta* which is exceptionally hardy and which flowers a month earlier. *O. Solandri* should also be considered. This species bears yellow flowers from August to October.

Pittosporum crassifolium is a shy flowerer but when it does, the purple flowers are exceptionally fragrant. This species is evergreen and is suitable for a taller hedge.

Veronica speciosa covers a large number of hybrids, ranging from blue, through the purples, to red in colour and flowering during the late summer; all are suitable for hedge work in sheltered districts.

Ceratostigma Willmottianum with its loose heads of deep blue flowers in August and September, is also suitable in a sheltered locality. This species will make a 2 ft. hedge.

Thus one can see that the choice is very much wider than many people imagine.

CHAPTER X

Climbers and Wall Shrubs

I HAVE already dealt with the subject of climbing shrubs suitable for the side of the house or to grow over a porch or pergola in the appropriate seasonal chapters. However, it would seem to be sensible to refer to them again, if only by name, in a separate chapter, at the same time affording me a chance to mention one or two extra species.

This is a book on flowering shrubs and trees and therefore I don't propose to expound on the virtues of such subjects as Ivy or Virginia Creeper.

Before allowing climbing plants to clothe the walls of any structure one must ensure that the brickwork, woodwork, etc., is in a first class state of repair. Even so, architects and builders will invariably advise against their use.

Turning now to the plants themselves, my list is not in any particular order.

Hydrangea petiolaris will climb to a height of 60 ft. bearing large, flat corymbs of white flowers in June.

Campsis radicans is a self-clinging climber suitable for a south wall. It bears tubular, orange-red, trumpet flowers during the summer. *Clematis* provides many species, several of which have been discussed earlier. Broadly speaking the hybrids are more satisfactory and give a wider range of colours than the species.

Wisteria sinensis should only be undertaken by those who intend it for a lifetime of pleasure. It needs careful training in the initial stage and an annual (August) pruning of unwanted shoots.

Lonicera × *americana* and varieties of *L. periclymenum* are ideal climbing Honeysuckles for archways and porches. Both are deciduous. There is also *L. japonica* which is evergreen and possesses fragrant flowers.

Jasminum nudiflorum and *J. officinale* have been referred to in earlier chapters, also *Kerria japonica, Campsis chinensis* and *Abutilon megapotamicum.*

Chimonanthus praecox is useful for its fragrant yellow flowers borne on bare stems in December and January.

Choisya ternata bears starry white, scented flowers in May. Both the last two species will reach 9 or 10 ft. in height.

Azara microphylla is another winter flowering species, offering its tiny fragrant flowers in February.

Chaenomeles japonica is a useful shrub to train against the wall, though it has no pretensions of being a climber.

Cotoneaster horizontalis and *C. microphylla* both bear brilliant scarlet berries from October to December.

Forsythia is another genus which will train well against the wall. This too has been discussed earlier in these pages.

Most of the above species will require carefully supporting and this fact must constantly be borne in mind.

111

Needless to say there are many other plants suitable as climbers or for use against a wall. Those given above are to my mind the cream of the possibles, though I do not discuss any members of the rose family in this book and they must, of course, not be forgotten.

CHAPTER XI

Landscaping

GARDEN landscapes cannot be designed with the use of the tape measure any more than the landscape artist will use a ruler when composing his pictures. The judgement and layout must be one for the eye alone, as it is the eye that we set out to please when preparing a landscape garden.

There is a scientific side to landscape gardening as well as the artistic side. The science involves the selection of the right plants and their maintenance. We must be very sure that we plant the right species and varieties in the right places. One probably has to live with one's garden for a long time. Planted correctly the right species will become dearly beloved friends but the wrong species — or the right ones planted in the wrong places — will provide a constant reminder of slothful planning or slipshod work.

As we are only dealing with shrubs and trees in

the landscape to the exclusion of flowers, there are certain principles which must be borne in mind by the small gardener when designing his layout. First of all his garden is complementary to his house and therefore the house must be considered as an integral part of the garden. This is not so difficult as it sounds because a house can be cloaked in such glorious subjects as Wisteria, Clematis, Jasmine, Rambling Roses and all the other delightful climbing plants.

The next point to consider is that one probably has neighbours that one usually wants to shut out, thus ensuring privacy. Yet at the same time one does not wish to be offensive and take all the neighbours' light. Nor should one plant subjects of which the roots will penetrate the neighbours' garden and rob his soil of all its goodness.

The third point with a small garden is the frontage which will probably butt on to the pavement. Again, one must decide whether or not prying eyes are to be defeated by tall growing shrubs and trees or whether they should be allowed complete freedom to gaze at the garden — or perhaps a combination of the two.

The fourth point to consider is the desirability of blocking out the sight of some particularly offensive architectural monstrosity from one's living room window. Perhaps there is an ugly factory chimney in view. This can be blocked out by a carefully sited, tall-growing, evergreen tree. Or a long line of buildings can be hidden by means of some of the more spreading types of tree and shrub; it is a good plan for the would-be garden designer, to know the shapes that are available

Finally the fifth principle is the importance of constantly bearing in mind the ultimate size to which the proposed subjects will grow. In this connection it is best to plant our selected trees and shrubs at the correct distances apart — and as a very rough guide the space required is the same as the ultimate height. This will naturally cause a number of gaps in the initial stages of growth. These gaps should be filled up, as a temporary measure, either by tall growing plants or less valuable shrubs, etc., that one is prepared to dispense with when the main subjects advance towards maturity. Never should one plant the main selections too close together, as there will be a reluctance to remove them later and they will never achieve the form and splendour they ought, due to the proximity of other subjects during the important shaping stage of their growth.

When growing flowers in the garden, particularly when one is considering the 'front' garden, there is usually — though not always, I am thankful to say — a tendency to rely on a certain amount of formality in the plan. With flowering shrubs this formality is absolutely out of the question and those who desire it should dismiss a shrub garden from their mind. The beauty of it lies in the informality of design.

Having discussed the principles, let us turn to the construction of the plan. Here it is helpful if we divide each section to be planted into nine parts. The three furthest away are called the background and must consist of those subjects designed to block out certain features, to shut out prying eyes or to act as a foil to the plants nearer the front. For this reason they will generally consist of evergreen species. The middle three are the most important features of the shrub garden. It is to the centre that the eye is generally drawn first. In this section should be the principle range of colour — though colour and season are vital in every part of the plan. They may be evergreen or deciduous.

If one of the background subjects chosen is deciduous it will be usual to include an evergreen or two in front of it. The front section of three divisions is used for the smaller species, generally rounded and bushy in habit and these are designed, not only to provide colour but to hide the trunks and stems of the larger species and to break up the outline of the subjects behind them.

Working now from side to side, naturally it will depend upon the size of the area under consideration but each section A, B, or C, must be treated as a separate unit consisting of species covering as many months of the year as possible. At the same time one must obviously avoid putting all the, say, summer flowering species in the front or central sections so that all the colours appear at once in the same line.

Some people like to arrange a bed so that everything is in flower at once. Though this method will offer a glorious display, to my mind it is fundamentally wrong, as with everything in flower at once, it is quite impossible to enjoy the full beauty of any single species, which can be done if for example, only the Laburnum or the Fuchsia is in flower at one time. The other species will still be beautiful — all nature's subjects are beautiful until spoiled by man — as there is coloured foliage, coloured stems and even the spring time beauty of bursting buds, all of which will enhance the loveliness of whatever species are in flower.

When one sets out to plan a similar bed with the house as a background, the background section will generally consist of climbers placed in strategic points either to cover a bare wall or to cloak a porchway, etc. Then the centre and front sections must consist of correspondingly suitable, dwarf species designed to fill the gaps, yet to avoid shutting the light out from a window or masking the beauty of the climbers. Near the house an emphasis should always be laid on the question of fragrance.

In the same way, when one sets the framework to a garden bed which is backed by the neighbour's fence, this fact can be taken into consideration and the necessity for evergreen shrubs will diminish — though evergreen tree species may still be useful to break outline and deter those prying eyes from 'snooping' over the fence.

When selecting subjects from chapters 5, 6, 7 and 8 for planting, one must remember that where one can make do with a small tree or shrub it may well allow room for another to flower at a different season, whereas a large subject would only allow the one and the consequent single season of bloom.

At the sides of a drive or on both sides of an entrance gate one should aim at symmetry, as great differences in size here will give a lopsided effect. This symmetry should not be provided by two of the same species. Two of a kind will seldom grow alike nor mature together and what may have started in symmetrical form may well end up as being very far from it.

Where a garden path is to be included as an integral part of the landscape feature, it should be a well designed and adequate path, perfectly suitable for the traffic it is expected to cater for, and above all it should never be straight.

DITION